Songs Presidential

Songs Presidential

Poems by

Jonathan Clark Patrick

© 2022 Jonathan Clark Patrick. All rights reserved.
This material may not be reproduced in any form, published,
reprinted, recorded, performed, broadcast,
rewritten or redistributed without
the explicit permission of Jonathan Clark Patrick.
All such actions are strictly prohibited by law.

Cover design by Shay Culligan

ISBN: 978-1-63980-123-7
Library of Congress Control Number: 2020475570

Kelsay Books
502 South 1040 East, A-119
American Fork, Utah 84003
Kelsaybooks.com

YOU just maturing youth! You male or female!
Remember the organic compact of These States,
Remember the pledge of the Old Thirteen thenceforward to the rights, life, liberty, equality of man,
Remember what was promulged by the founders, ratified by The States, signed in black and white by the Commissioners, and read by Washington at the head of the army,
Remember the purposes of the founders,—Remember Washington;
Remember the copious humanity streaming from every direction toward America;
Remember the hospitality that belongs to nations and men; (Cursed be nation, woman, man, without hospitality!)
Remember, government is to subserve individuals,
Not any, not the President, is to have one jot more than you or me,
Not any habitan of America is to have one jot less than you or me.

Anticipate when the thirty or fifty millions, are to become the hundred, or two hundred millions, of equal freemen and freewomen, amicably joined.

Recall ages—One age is but a part—ages are but a part . . .

"Poem of Remembrance of a Girl or a Boy"

—Walt Whitman

Acknowledgment

I would like to acknowledge Zack Rogow without whose editorial help and personal support I would not have been able to finish this work.

And I would like to acknowledge the perseverance of the historians whose research and commitment to uncovering, understanding and recording the facts of the past inspired me to focus on the American presidency.

Abraham Lincoln photograph by Alexander Gardner, November 1863

Barack Obama photograph—US President Barack Obama speaks during a town hall meeting on Health Insurance at Central High School in Grand Junction, Colorado, USA on August 15, 2009. Photo by Olivier Douliery/ABACAPRESS.COM

Contents

Remembrance of a Man, Then a Boy	13
Whitman	14
The Mill of the Stars	15
Making Butter	16
The Edge of the Frontier	17
The Limits of Transcendentalism	18
The American Dark Ages	19
Deaths Foretold	20
1860 Lincoln	21
1865 Johnson	26
1868 Grant	28
1876 Hayes	32
1880 Garfield	34
1881 Arthur	36
1884 Cleveland	38
1888 Harrison	41
1892 Cleveland	43
1896 McKinley	44
1901 Roosevelt	47
1908 Taft	52
1912 Wilson	53
1920 Harding	55
1923 Coolidge	57
1928 Hoover	59
1932 Roosevelt	61
1945 Truman	66
1952 Eisenhower	68
1960 Kennedy	72
1963 Johnson	76
1968 Nixon	78
1974 Ford	83
1976 Carter	85

1980 Reagan	88
1988 Bush	92
1992 Clinton	95
2000 Bush	98
2008 Epilogue Obama	101

Remembrance of a Man, Then a Boy

The garden, the wooden-handled spade
Slipping from his ungloved hands, calloused,
The Man in confusion,
His left arm tingling, breathless,
Bizarrely hungry, curious,
The burden of the pain in his chest.

Wobbly, worried, fearing the worst,
Wanting to press through the blindness.

A voice rummaging for facts, first name, birth date,
Tang of nitroglycerin bitters,
The under-slide of the backboard
Hefting him to the stretcher,
Sirens, strobes red and white.

Signing unreadable releases
In the shadow of chattering surgeons,
Their quarreling incomprehensible.

Resurrection, woke and wired, connected.

The Man indentured to his treadmill,
Reparations for decades of neglect,
Listening to the poems the Boy loved,
Walt's songs, blind Milton's arguments,
Homer and Virgil, creation myths,
Accepting Walt's prescript to read history,
To know the Founding Fathers.

And so the Man set out to read.

Whitman

I see the whole long years of him.
The boy in Long Island fields
And the farms of ancestors
Or Brooklyn shanties—builder's son
Red flannel shirt exposed at the neck, darkly bearded,
Wool coat and rough trousers
Tucked into farmer's boots.
Risen boy to smooth-shaven man,
His Long Island years teaching,
The tar, the feathers, remembered.
Now gray-beard, the Rebellion done,
Sweet Walt in dark suit and soul-white shirt
Finally, chair-bound, skin translucent, then abed withering.
Soon the Corpse long rotted in Camden fields
Entombed with mother and father, brothers and sisters,
Boy come to man, come to earth.

And I see myself, Boy to Man,
Judge my own path,
The Boy in New Hampshire, Silver Lake in August,
First-light fog unmoved by the midday drone of horseflies,
The persistent chill surrendered without complaint
Sun cresting the pine-pricked White Mountains.
Gray, gray, gray water and sky—the dappled plane of the lake
Caddis flies emergent in ripples concentric, intersecting.
And so history, a surface in motion.

The Mill of the Stars

Whitman and the Boy,
The water-frame
Stretched, the warp of History,
Witness to the weft whipped,
Left to Right, Right to Left,
Flying shuttle caressed
By the calloused hands
Of New England mill girls.

So reputations,
As if calico stars
Woven into broadloom,
In the gloaming of Manchester Mills,
Patterns and prints, machined,
Mechanic in hindsight,
The Mill of the Stars.
We witnessed
The jacquard intent in the weave,
The revelation in the cloth.

Making Butter

At the edge of the world.
The Northwest bank of the Ohio,
Ohi-yo, "Good River,"
Frontier Women making butter in Marietta,
Hands swollen pulling warm milk
From teats of Holsteins driven
Out of New England farms to the Territory,
Rafted on flat boats from civilized Pittsburgh
South and West, swallowed whole,
So many Jonahs in the Wilderness.
Churning, shaking or plunging,
Cream separated and skimmed,
Worked by field-bruised hands
Into butter-bricks cooled in springhouses.

In the Boy's century,
Nashoba Valley, New England,
Mother Dot, uniformed, starched whites,
Serving school lunches:
Fish sticks, dogs and burgers,
Baked beans, chips or slaw;
Stirring meat sauce salted
And chili-peppered for sloppy joes,
Shredding lettuce, grating cheddar,
Slicing tomatoes and red onions;
At the register taking quarters.
The Boy paying his mother for lunch
With the spare change she gave him that morning.

The Edge of the Frontier

*The Boy, Saturday morning roaming
The pine woods hemming Fort Pond Brook,
Emerging from the wood ferns, tall as he,
Jurassic their reek, into meadows sunlit.
The Boy imagined himself, fixed in the sun's glower,
Whipping oxen out of the Missouri Woods,
Onto the Nebraska Plains, the Platte Sandhills,
To choose Northwest and the Oregon Trail
Or Southwest to Santa Fe, then California.*

*In his century, accepting the marsh grass scratches,
The horseflies humming, the stench of the wet ground,
The thatch of grass and root, the rot.
At the pooling brook, standing on trembling hummocks,
Spiny-finned catfish aimless in the black-green water weeds.
A boy's tackle box opened at his feet,
A disorder of barbs and filament, weights and floats
Acquired as his allowance allowed at Laughlin's Hardware.
Balled bread spit-glued to the barb lead weighted,
A hornpout hooked and cranked into the air,
Secured beneath a green-sneakered foot,
Wet and blackened with mud,
The hook free, the fish strung,
Home for butter and salt, pan-fried.*

The Limits of Transcendentalism

The Boy, twelve, ascending Nashoba oaks,
Thoreau's shed a day's hike East at Concord,
Close upon Old North Bridge, Alcott's Fruitlands
West of Emerson's manse on the Turnpike.

The Boy prefiguring the Man's world,
Thinly muscled arms embracing
Immature limbs nearest the spinning spheres,
A confident red-tailed raptor preening, hopeful.

In the age before the communal fling with Nature,
East, Puritan Salem and Witches on Crucifixes;
West, Sinners swooning in clapboard churches,
Edwards singing of Spiders in the Pioneer Valley.

And in the gloaming of Concordia's decline,
South and West, armies belligerent,
Age begets Age, persistent.

The American Dark Ages

After Polk—manifest hero of Mexico,
Taylor, Fillmore, Pierce, indolent Buchanan,
Men of the twelve dark years before the war
Wallowing amid schemes so darkly political
As if green weeds combed by sullen currents
Running cold beneath black ice.

In Nashoba, the valley in winter,
My self, a boy with plaid cap,
Venturing the frozen brook,
Kneeling to sweep away the morning snow,
Seeing through the black ice
The wild weeds, cold,
Anchored to the scoured bottom,
Presidents of the slow current,
Electors of the bend in the river,
Weeds content to writhe, to swerve, and gyre
For the ice now lensing the January sun—no thawing
Until April comes to Nashoba.

Deaths Foretold

The Man, the Boy auguring
From the entrails of biography
Nurse Walt nomadic,
Pallet rows, pyramids of limbs
Sawed, gutters blooded,
The Nightingales, aprons soiled,
The ruined boys incoherently moaning,
Columns of Brothers
Exploited by God
And Manmade Machines,
Victims of Generals obeyed,
Dying all the same,
In victory or defeat,
Science not quite ready for Soldiering
In the Nineteenth Century
Despite Nurses courageous.

1860 Lincoln

Confronting the ill-omened limits of America,
Grief bound ruined and extended families,
A Mother surrendered to milk sickness,
A Sister in giving birth, a Grandfather scalped,
The Frontier reinforcing survivors' resolve,
To prevail despite Providence.

Out of the Northwest Territories,
Frontier-nurtured in the American Dark Ages,
Looking to the Founders and the heft of precedent.
Lincoln, a self-made seventh son
Of Hingham England Lincolns,
Immigrants to Hingham, Massachusetts,
Puritans Westward coveting new territories.

Out of land-bound Kentucky,
Diaspora to Indiana's first-growth forest,
Reading Washington's story
In a Wilderness his father made no better.
Following his own Westward journey,
Obsessed with Illinois prairies, free soil.
A rough man, a giant,
Wrestler, Reader, Storyteller,
Melancholic, moody, despairing
That the Necessity of the body politic
Would sweep Reason downriver.
And he, enslaved to Fate,
Was on his own curious flatboat,
Steering-oar carving the brown current,
A one-way passage to a New Orleans auction.

A young man, raw-boned
No stranger to Slavery,
Still, Innocent,
Coming to Age downriver,
His goods and flatboat sold,
Roving New Orleans streets
Ruled by slave pens,
Chained slaves scourged
In their nakedness
Suffering the indifference
Of auctioneers, buyers and pious tourists.

No political bumpkin, Spotty Lincoln,
Surveyor and Post Office manager,
Lawyer, State Rep, Congressman,
A Westerner who wouldn't be bullied,
Famous in opposition to Little Giant Douglas,
The Kentucky log cabin a long, long time ago.

Working free of the collar tie
Of Taylor, Fillmore, Pierce,
The Union sacrificed to Buchanan's perfidy,
And now, Everyman forced to choose a tribe.
Abe, will you wear, honestly,
The black cape of the Wide-Awakes?
Parade Springfield's cobbles, newly laid,
With Union Shriekers and Rail-splitters?
Or take the Blue Secesh Cockade
And with your Cavalier fire-eater cousins
Parade the Charleston Battery?

Abe, a sure bet in a wrestling match,
Awkwardly shouldered command
Those first few months of rebellion.
A Confederacy of nine states
Already a hostile foreign nation
A month before he took office;
Sumter seized and four more states
Seceding within his first month, soon thirteen,
One third of the states forsaking union;
Countless skirmishes for armories and forts,
Small prizes lost along the new border.
Abe, believing in discourse and reason,
Overwhelmed by the rush to rebellion
And its price in blood.

In '62, Abe, confronting Oblivion,
Wrapped in a homespun shawl, striped black,
Rocking away his grief, weeping,
In the unhappy rooms of his House
His third son Willie dead of typhoid,
Cradling young Tad, Mary beyond consolation—
No auguries of the Titan
Commanding the Capitol in the Boy's century
Atop Colorado marble steps,
Within memorial walls joined of limestone
And pink granite from North and South.
Twenty-three thousand causalities, Blue & Gray,
Offered for Shiloh Church;
On the Peninsular, traitor McClellan,
His grand army retreating
South by Southeast until Malvern Hill,

Thirty-five thousand fallen in seven inglorious days;
A stalemate at Antietam, twenty-two thousand lost
After all-day battles contesting a cornfield,
A sluggish brown creek, a sunken country road,
A one-room Dunker church, its solitary wood stove cold;
Luckless Burnside blundering into Fredericksburg,
Seventeen thousand fallen,
The Blue boys crying through the snowy night
At the foot of Marie's Heights.

Father Abraham wrestling with God's purpose,
Both sides claiming righteousness,
Both sides could be wrong, one side surely wrong,
What was God's intent in exacting
Sacrifices measured in hectares of blood?
All men having been created equal,
Surely God must side with the Emancipator.
The People bewildered by two years of losses.
Lincoln bemoaning the Lost, "What will the Country say?"
Defeat cloaking the Capitol
Until he, pressed by armies living off the land,
Foraging the sprawling plantations,
The first time, many a New England Boy
Saw a Black Man, freed or not,
And Northern abolitionists determined
To bring Hard War to the Rebels,
Enlisted fleeing Contraband,
Confiscated Rebel property,
Emancipated the Southern Slaves.

God demanded War
Between North and South
For the offense of slavery,
So Abe declared, a month shy of Appomattox,
Blood drawn by the lash, repaid by the sword.

And that last euphoric moment,
Lincoln in his rocker laughing,
Wilkes-Booth behind him, cloaked,
Determined to alter history.

Fifth Grade, the Boy as Lincoln
In the Presidents' Day Pageant.
Dot sewed his waistcoat from a homemade pattern,
Fashioning a stovepipe hat, fitting black silk
On a frame she made from shirt cardboards
And reworked into brim and crown.
The Boy sacrificing himself
Before the Grades and Families assembled.

What was the dream
The traitor's bullet spoiled?
Fairness, forgiveness?
Lost to the ages, unlike the man.

1865 Johnson

Volunteer Johnson, unelected,
Tailor-boy, "low-born" tyro,
Fled west from Carolina's hills at seventeen
Sewing his grudges into a winding sheet
Like Copperheads in a snake-bag.
Racism the very heart of him,
Nurtured in the Tennessee hollows,
The cold green Cumberland gullies,
Where thousands would fall
In Blue and Gray works at Shiloh Church
And Missionary Ridge, in his mind—all for nothing.

Pardoned the Cotton Princes he claimed to hate,
Shackled the freedman to ploughshare law
Through Regulator and Black Codes
And indifference to the lynch-fever he loosed.
So anxious to rewrite history—for Whites Only!
Striving to restore, not reconstruct the South.
His hateful intent thwarted by impeachment,
And his short-lived censorious Senate resurrection,
While Freedmen in patched cotton blouses
Demanded suffrage and ownership of fields
They had cleared for their pardoned Masters.

The Boy, growing up in colorless Nashoba,
A freshman in college, unworldly,
When first introduced to boys and girls of color
From urban neighborhoods or road's end
In hill counties or Southern Lowlands;
Life experiences he could barely grasp,
Knowing something of farms and working poor,
But nothing of the streets painted in nightly newscasts.

Johnson's winding sheet a Union Flag,
His personal Constitution, his casket pillow,
Wherein, amid the worms,
He rots speechless,
Bones bleached white,
Alone.

The Boy graduated,
Driving for Town Taxi,
Garaged in the shadow
Of Fenway's Green Monster.
The city machinery
Corrupt, Boston failing,
Government free falling,
Forced bussing, tribalism,
Hate corroding the body politic,
The ample throat of hell obvious.
In those opaque years,
Sometimes writing,
Not for causes glorious
But to convince himself
He mattered,
He was not alone.

1868 Grant

Ulysses Grant—apocalypse himself,
General of the Army Potomac.
Emancipating, offensive legions unerring,
Advancing on a bloody flood-tide of battles.
Surrender unconditional, U.S. Grant.

His biographers and memoirs opaque
To binges and bones broken, hangovers,
The lack of discipline, a sip, a taste,
A reckless night-ride crazed on Kentuck' rye.

Our love informed by battles lost and won,
Grant sat his bay horse, no matter the loss.

Brother Ed, board game savant,
Playing Battle Cry tournaments
On the deck of the Massachusetts
A thousand leagues, decades safe
From the Marshalls and Okinawa.
The Boy never able to best him
Whether given North or South.
Brother, general of the dice
And the hexagonal squares
Of advance and retreat,
Owning the outcome,
If South, outlast the Blue,
Hope for British interdiction;
If North, crush the Rebellion,
No quarter, no compromise!

After that bloody day at Shiloh,
When Prentiss and Wallace manned the Hornet's Nest,
The Army in flight to the Tennessee,

Sherman's 5th held Johnston and Beauregard
South of Pittsburg under the Union gunships,
Buell steaming across the river under cover of Night,
Grant whispering to Sherman
Despairing, spent after the assault,
"Lick 'em tomorrow."

Vicksburg seized after the dark advance
Through Mississippi bayou and backswamp,
Given general command of the Army,
And, in Virginia, by the left flank
After the Wilderness toward Richmond,
Countless dead at Spotsylvania,
Yellow Tavern, Meadow Bridge, North Anna,
Cold Harbor, always flanking south-southeast,
Stars pinned to a soldier's blouse, General.

Petersburg and Richmond fallen, Retreat,
To Danville, Lee's flight, Sailor's Creek, Farmville,
The Courthouse siege, the dead, the deserters,
Barefoot, hungry men, censored, defeated.
The Army of Northern Virginia paroled,
To take up the Lost Cause.

By '68, Black Renaissance, crossroad stores
Bartering seed-stock, cotton ginned, wool spun,
A black economy, black-belt parishes and schools,
Families impoverished by sharecropping, but Black
And free, voting, owning the land they worked,
Elected judges, sheriffs, and congressmen.

Grant careless in his Cabinet choices,
Content to let the Republican machine
Fill the purses of Northern carpetbaggers,
Syphoning the treasury, stuffing
Saddlebags and valises,
Corruption in every district, precinct, ward,
A presidency of grifters,

"Redeemed" confederates remade the South,
And costumed Night Riders settled old scores
In hoods and homespun blouses bleached
White as raw cotton bolls field-ginned, red-crossed,
Lynched Freedmen and Scallywags,
Torched Black schools, whipped Quakers raw,
Suppressed the Black man's vote,
Impressed again White privilege.
In the tobacco and sugar kingdoms,
The cotton plantations, the rice lowlands,
Reconstruction's green shoots yanked as field weeds.

Northern Corporations emancipated
From their regulators, began their march
To Citizenship, the Gilded Age blooming
In Beacon Hill, Park Avenue, Knob Hill.
While Federal troops, freed from Southern policing,
Instead, broke Unions at the bidding of Railroad lobbyists
The Armies now occupying the Northeast,
And hunting the Nez Perce in the Northwest.

At Balmoral dying in his bath chair,
Pencil talk with Julia, his voice given over
To cancer, Adirondacks beckoning,
General Grant destitute, desperate.

Penning memoirs, saving heirs the poorhouse,
General of the Armies at the mercy
Of strangers, a ghoulish attraction
For moneyed Saratoga horsemen,
In columns parading up McGregor's Hill,
Staring the frail man, national savior,
Into the impatient earth he bloodied.

1876 Hayes

Heir to War Gods in a Corrupt Age,
President Rudd, polite, honest enough,
Preferred the company of Poets,
Devoted to Longfellow and Emerson,
Ignoring the age of Black Codes
And Southern vendettas against equality
Ushered in by his compromised election.

In the War's infancy,
Suspicious of Lincoln,
Favoring a nation divided
As long as one was Free.
Marched with Crook in the Cumberland,
And doomed McKinley's Ohio 23rd,
With Pope at Bull Run routed, Burnside at Antietam Creek;
And Little Phil in the Valley against Early.

After Freedmen votes were cancelled
By shadow Confederate governments
In Florida, Louisiana, and Corrupt Carolina,
The election disputed,
The determined South holding
The deciding College votes,
Elected by Commission
With a promise to put down Reconstruction.

The Man considered Hayes' entrails,
Augured his own character.
Would he have chosen to sacrifice
The Freedmen for the chimera of Union?

Baffling, Rudd's Planter Aristocracy restoration
And the murder of Reconstruction.
Indifferent to Black Laws and lynching,
Self-deluded he had healed the Nation,
Birthing five generations of white supremacy,
Disenfranchisement, black families,
In oral histories, recalling those few years
When equality was a thing, possible.
Hayes, thinking himself sacrificed for Union,
But his reputation as War-ruined
As the thousands of soldiers' bodies
Blue and Gray blouses and britches
Torn to rags by canister shot.

1880 Garfield

Garfield, log cabin born and farm poor,
Forty acres of dust and corn, father gone
And Eliza determined to educate her son
Who grew into a stern, bearded man,
Field-hand strong, driving mules dragging canal boats,
Come to learning as a last resort, excelling.

Infinite as the spheres that spin, his possibilities
In those days before the Kentucky fights
When General Garfield drove the rebels
Out of Lincoln's birthplace, Union earned.

Garfield, more capable than Hayes or Grant,
Heir to the Emancipator, a teacher
And Senator from the Northwest Frontier
Drafted by disaffected delegates
Looking for Stalwart alternatives.
At Chicago come to speak for Sherman's brother,
Not the best Sherman nor the best candidate.
Garfield, the best in us, our promise.

Country doctors operating in their Sunday suits,
Unsheathing iron instruments, crudely fashioned,
From leather bags stained from past interventions,
Ignoring Lister, infected hands and tools
Violating saintly Garfield's body.

The Boy desperate to be Garfield
Tortured for the Republic,
Victim of witch doctors,
Dying as he looked Eastward
From Jersey's Shore,

Not quite Paumanok,
The Boy heard Walt's whisper,
"In Him all the Leaves Heroic!"

Assassin Guiteau goaded by God,
Convinced he was protagonist
In Garfield's victory, reward unrealized,
Stalked the President, resolved to murder,
To elevate Stalwart Arthur, executive.
Guiteau to Glory, or so he imagined,
Until the rope cut short his poetry, his singing,
Voice from thought, spine from will, swinging.

1881 Arthur

Stalwart Arthur, not The King,
Puppet of spoiling bosses,
Preening for power and lucre,
Made President by God,
His chapel hand, Guiteau.

Born handsome, swaddled
In abolitionist verses chanted
By a fanatic preacher-father.

A corpulent, mannered Prince of his Age,
Welcoming debauchery,
Fond of broad cloth suits,
Morgan horses, broughams,
And Low Country cigars.

Arthur—his Nellie undone by diphtheria,
Grieving and bequeathed a nation speechless,
Garfield done in by sepsis.

A career man practiced,
Machine-made, machine maker,
Corrupted, corruptor,
Unequal to his moment,
Unable to write his history
Albeit holding the inked quill.

Oblivious to the reformer's miter,
Neither priest nor president,
With a phantom congregation.
Unable, unwilling to pledge
A future state garlanded
In the raw colors of Reform.

Mortal Arthur,
Given up reelection,
Realizing damnation,
Sins unconfessed, unforgiven,
Political papers burned,
A vainglorious proffer to expunge
A career of profiteering.

The Man anxious
Over chances certainly squandered
In adolescence selfishly pursued.
Was He another false Arthur
Unable to merit Choruses
Inherit a magic sword, a magician?

1884 Cleveland

Child of Mass Bay Preachers,
Uncle Jumbo, philanderer,
Conscripted, hired a Polish Émigré
To fight his fight
In the Rebellion that made Presidents.

Buffalo hangman, Sheriff Cleveland
Wobbling between saloons,
Grail sloshing with warm Upstate ale.

"Where's my Pa?"
Teased the broadsheets,
Orphaned son,
Grover the Good
"Gone to the White House
Hah, Ha, Ha!"

Marrying Frances, she'll do.

A Big Man, a career man with appetites.
Bourbon Democrat in thrall to railroad trusts.
An Insurance Man's Administration,
Mr. Status Quo?
Indifferent to Sioux extermination
Or Southern lynching.

She stands before you, Lucy Parsons,
Anarchist, begging pennies
From Grover's Gilded Army
For doomed and dandy Parsons
Almost two years in prison,
An advocate of violence, a labor martyr,
A hanged man, a talker.

For decades after, Lucy in union halls,
At picnic rallies, on Chicago's cold street curbs,
Blood Drinker and Dynamiter, retelling their story.

The Boy-Man cab driver and poet,
Writing sonnets to radicals of the 60s,
Recorded on cassette
And replayed, reworked, yearning to sing.
A raw, untutored voice,
Whitman in his heart and head,
Wanting that, in letters to his artist friend.

A wonder Jumbo became President,
Did little to earn re-election.
In '88 losing to the dandy Harrison
All of five-foot-six counting his stovepipe hat.
The Little General, made by the War,
Reconstruction Republican,
Spoiling and righteous.

The Boy-Man working
For Brother Ed, earnestly,
MBA at night, poetry in the drawer,
A career man, closeting the rebel,
Closeting the placards of the 70s
Stop The Bombing,
A Little Peace Never Hurt No One!

And so many self-made Brigadiers,
A century earlier, gone home,
Restocking dry-goods, weighing soybeans,
Wrapping stone-ground flour in brown paper,

Selling hand-wrought nails by the pennyweight
For repairing roofs, fences and cow barns;
Clerking in territorial banks, processing
Loans to veterans purchasing bottom land;
Stoking coke in steel furnaces,
Or drilling deep in coal mines,
Driving locomotives, steering flatboats.

Assent after Shiloh, Antietam,
Gettysburg, Farmville and Sailor's Creek,
They, once heroic, now transformed,
Both newborn and timeworn as the fields
That witnessed their struggle.
Time to move on, to work and build.

1888 Harrison

Benjamin, grandson of Tippecanoe
And great-grandson of Tidewater Harrison,
A Signer, ancestry indentured to Jamestown,
His forbearers, the white-pine sap of Virginia.

Sunday School teacher, Psalm-follower,
One of many Indiana men
On the Road to Atlanta with Sherman;
And with Thomas in Cumberland's bloodied woods,
Where the Confederates in the West at last fell.

In the wake of the Victors,
Ben, having earned his Brigadier stars,
Marching north through wretched, wrecked Richmond,
The Chancellorsville defile,
The Wilderness, twice blooded,
Re-fording the Rappahannock,
Retracing the marches
Of the Army of the Potomac,
Burying the Union Dead,
Years rotting in the battlefields,
Mile upon hallowed haunted mile,
Until the unfinished Capitol,
Rising into the May sky as gray as Lee's blouse,
Took their breath away, glorious.

Campaigning from his porch,
Victor, squandering the popular vote.

Unworthy of the Centennial,
Oblivious to Wounded Knee,
And the Johnstown victims
Of Mercantilist Wall Street;

Focused on Patronage, Silver and Tariffs,
Another man risen high but unwilling
To preserve the Rights of all.

Finally, corpulent Ben empowered,
Insider, in an Age of Insider Trading,
Owning Waterworks and Coal Mines,
And silver deposits in the Nevada hills.
Admitting the Dakotas
Wyoming, Idaho and Washington,
Montana mines and mining.
O Oklahoma!
Conestoga wagons retracing
The Trail of Tears,
Obliterating the Native traces.
Harrison of Manifest Destiny,
Relentless, his advance to the Western Sea
Four years managing the "White Man's Burden."

The Man, in remembrance,
Of the Boy desperate
For the soldier-hero Grant
Or the martyred Lincoln,
Saw in Harrison, a mechanic.
The Boy wanted stories of heroes
Ferried by Charon, the still Styx,
Hymns, songs, regimental pennants,
Glory spilt on hill after hill,
The sorrow-filled abattoirs, the dead
Entrenched behind pine abatis,
Soldiers' sacrifices,
And heroes' corpses on catafalques,
Draped in black and white silk.

1892 Cleveland

Uncle Jumbo restored in '92,
Enthralled by Fall River Lizzie, her Axe,
Inheriting the Socialist Debs,
Unable to serve his countrymen or country,
Paralyzed by the Panic of '93.

Uncle Jumbo squandering
Second chances, unable to profit
From Populism, Progressivism, Anarchism,
Assassins and terrorists in training in the 90s.
Our Uncle Jumbo, do nothing Bag of Beef
Except when Pullman called
To sacrifice Union Men in Haymarket,
Lucy and Albert protesting Labor's lost causes.

Gilded Age Barons
Carousing in the White House,
Albeit Jumbo tried to do what he thought was right,
When he could focus beyond his cravings,
Grover the Good, in his own mind.

The Man and Boy saw,
Like so many fathers and sons,
In Grover the Good, a well-intended princeling,
Whose sack cloth coat and top hat indifference
To self-improvement, the body-politic,
Or any cause save gluttony,
Would be buried with him,
His the shortest of presidential songs.

1896 McKinley

"Boys don't let them hurt Him!"

Slumped in his Temple chair,
Re-elected barely a year,
Czolgosz done his murdering duty,
The Gilded Age dead, buried.

Last of the Civil War heroes,
Sweet McKinley of the Ohio 23rd
A kill-shot to the paunch,
Decades after the slaughter
Of so many Ohioans
At Burnside's Bridge.
Foretelling his Republican heirs,
Exploitation, conspicuous,
Of lands beyond the Americas,
As if an Old World Empire
Rather than a New World democracy
Only lately reunited as One.

A singular and thoughtful boy,
Leon, absorbed in boyish rhymes,
Wanting to make his mark,
Working the looms in Five Points
Assassin in the making, Anarchist.

The Boy, the Man, graduate,
Student and Assistant,
Researching Lawrence mill girls
For professors resolved to publish
Analyses of the poetry of girls
Shackled to looms

*In abolitionist New England,
Indentured property until married,
Returned to the farm, or buried.*

McKinley, bullying business,
The Southern masses toiling in the cane fields,
Allied with Sinclair's slaughterhouses,
A Gilded Age, tarnished,
McKinley offered and sacrificed.

Leon, a farm boy coveting independence,
Found his true way in the sulfurous
Beer hall speeches of heartland anarchists,
Man is Master, Individual, and Perfect!

Haymarket and the Property Beast!
For Leon, the martyr Parsons
"Will I be allowed to speak?"
Homestead and the Property Beast!
And Beckman at Frick's throat
In Carnegie's Steel Temple.

And golden-haired Czolgosz
Stalking Red Emma.
On the lookout for meetings,
A unit in the universe, anarchist,
Avowing the Propaganda of the Deed,
Assassination, the courage of the crime.
McKinley butchered like Garfield
By assassin and doctor poisoned.

"No one told me to do it.
I was not paid.
I was all stirred up and had to kill him
For the good of the laboring people."

So death by Electric Current,
And deportation for Emma,
Freighted to Russia in the Red Ark,
Sharing steerage with sympathetic socialists
Culled from *Mother Earth* subscription lists.
The time of Anarchists done.

From far Nashoba, the future,
The Man rereading what the Boy learned.
The challenge of storytelling,
McKinley, his time demanding,
Are public men born innocent
Of Lincoln's sacrifices and failings?
Where balances the teeter-totter soul
Of presidents flawed in hindsight
But principled enough in their own days?

1901 Roosevelt

New World Hercules
Teddy, tasked to cleanse,
A quarter century of New York rot,
Without the East nor Hudson Rivers re-routed.
Roosevelt, Colossus.

Promoter of Americanism, himself,
The man also the country becoming.
Americanism triumphant over Union.
Globalist Teddy, an American imperium,
Unimagined by Presidents before him,
Presiding over a nation his predecessors,
Save the few, underestimated, misled.

Walt empathetic to the cloistered child,
Manhattan raised, mansion-mannered,
Now a Man expansive, Emperor of the West!
Full figured rising, all chest and teeth,
Multiplying as we weighed him.
Roosevelt, dandy and cowboy,
White as Dutch New York,
Bronzed as Dakota plainsmen.
Historian and Hunter.
Teddy twittering, teeth clicking,
Four-eyed cowboy preaching Life is Strife.
Electric Teddy—Sparking and sparker, Rough Rider.
The most famous man in America!
Speaking softly, carrying a big stick,
His story his age.

The Boy in Nashoba,
No Dakota Territory rancher,

But a dreamer
Impatient for his monthly issues
Of Field and Stream, Outdoor Life,
Devouring the fishing sagas,
First-person narratives of quests for lake trout,
Bass – small and large mouthed,
Walleye and needle-toothed pickerel,
Imagining fly fishing in Montana or Alaska,
With streamers and dry flies, hand-tied,
In lakes cold and clear,
In rivers catholic after April thaw,
Experimenting with lures, spoons,
Poppers in obscure configurations,
Daredevils in red, black and yellow striping,
A dictionary of possibilities, fishing.
The Boy's Sears catalog exegesis,
As if a catechism memorized.

One Saturday, secretly and alone,
Liberating Eddie's split bamboo rod,
A ten-foot stretch of filament
Knotted to the top eyelet, no reel,
Jigging a feathered spinner, beaded,
Under the Boston and Maine trestle
Where Fort Pond Brook spilled transparent and chilled,
Into a careless distortion in the current,
Rainbows hovering, ecstatic in eddies stone-formed.
Furious Eddie,
Depression formed,
A hoarder, possessive.
Would not, could not, share.
The Boy, alone, cooking his catch.

Teddy and Muir, like teenage lovers,
Descending from Yosemite's glaciers
Arm-in-arm, come down, mountaineers
Teddy huge, Muir schoolgirl-small.

Teddy and Booker T., tête-à-tête, at Dinner
Unrepentant South aghast,
A Black Man in the White House,
Where slave owners gorged on carved meats
And downed juleps, debauched.
Where even Lincoln declined
To share a meal with the emancipated.

Panama, the sovereign scar, canal,
Teddy's gunboat diplomacy
Our 20th Century prelude.

Ocean to Ocean, sixteen dreadnoughts
White as American History,
The Great White Wall of armor steaming
The Radius and Diameter Equatorial
America Hemispheric, Global, finally.

In Africa nine months until sated on hearts of elephants,
Amateur scientist amid the gore and license,
The skin and ivory, the empty eye sockets awaiting glass marbles.

Then entangled in the Matto Grosso, fallen,
Kermit porting his father's fevered body
Through the anarchy of insects
And rot fallen from the canopies.

The Man kept the rod,
Eddie long buried in southeast New Hampshire scrabble
Beside Brother Henry, beneath a Celtic cross
Honoring his rope-maker Grandfather,
Highlands birthright abandoned in the 1850s
For Newfoundland, then Boston by 1910.
Aich! The Scots ken well British irons.

Dottie allowed the decades to pass
Her final wishes obscured
By Alzheimer phantoms,
And the Man's sisters and brothers
Deciding she would lie alone,
A Winter burial in the frost-hard earth
Of suburban Massachusetts,
A resting place Grace earned
For her children after decades of shifts,
In the Waltham factories,
After steaming to America in 1904.
Grace, nine, the oldest of five,
Fleeing the Empire's rationing
Of Cardiff commoners' dreams.
Her four sons and her daughter
Gifted with possibilities beyond the reveries
Of Welsh coal miners and slate quarrymen,
Owning a watch, an American watch,
Finished by immigrant hands,
Movement, clock face and bezel, given time.

Candidate in Perpetuity.
Himself, radiance leaking from a collapsing star,
The starlight of Colonel Roosevelt filtered by losses,
Son dead in war, preparedness for what?

Life is Strife, wanderlust for an enemy worthy of the fight.
The wanton craving
Of a sickly Manhattan boy
For the immortality of the Spartans,
The Eagles of the Caesars.
Roosevelt—the most famous man in the world!

1908 Taft

Will Taft, a placeholder,
His short-story presidency grist
Between millstones grinding fine:
Teddy, patron first then comic foe,
Woodrow, the president Will wished he was.

Imagine a President, later Chief Justice,
Dead in 1930, the depression dead on,
Defender of Wilson, the League and the 14 Points,
Imagine Will in the unforgiving winter of '31,
Imagine him in '39, Poland's sacrifice,
The murderous '40s of the Wehrmacht.

Proud of his first born, isolationist Robert?
Proud of the Hoover worshipper,
New Deal dissenter and WWII resister?
Did Will anticipate his son
Hating on Ike, beloved by Dick?

The Man reflecting on his own love
For his millennial sons, OK boomer.
Their journeys dissimilar, the age digital,
The failure of the Man and his generation
To renew the world, or at least America,
Informed or not by Eddie's postwar
Experience building a family
In the dreamy bubble of the '50s,
The greatest generation's legacy
Of systemic inequality simmering.
The Man looking back, hopeful,
But redemption as yet unearned
For Eddie the Father, or the Boy, the Son.

1912 Wilson

Professor Tommy's potential thwarted,
Roosevelt in death proved prophetic,
Preparedness, and the Big Stick of Americanism
Pedant Tommy, righteous and unpersuasive,
While Cassandra called from Oyster Bay.
Tommy Triumphant, the Great War won,
Pershing gassing Germanic hordes into Armistice.

A 20th century Prometheus
By the harpy eagles of the Senate set upon
Who fed on his pride while Death fed on him.

Unbent, alone and bankrupt,
Buried like the Westminster kings
In a marble sarcophagus
Sunlit by stained glass,
The National Cathedral,
Almost Catholic, and he the image
Of his Virginia Presbyterian Slaver forebears.
Entombed and impenetrable Tommy
In his way as tough as Teddy,
Although no plains rancher in buckskin and Stetson,
Hand caressing his holstered Colt,
But he only had the love of his women, not his people.

The Boy exploring in Grandma Grace's attic,
Uncovering his uncle's cache of Tom Swift novels
Reading, rereading, three decades removed
From Wilson's age of Hope and Terror,
Of Futurism and Science Fiction,
Of Self-Help and Invention.
The Boy In Captivity,

In The Land of Wonders *and* The City of Gold;
Imaging himself Tom, Boy Inventor
With His Giant Cannon, *His* Ariel Warship,
His War Tank *and* Flying Boat,
His Sky Train *and* Giant Telescope,
His Television Detector *and* Giant Magnet,
His Electric Locomotive *and* Wizard Camera.

Wilson's age,
And the age of Edison,
The Wright brothers,
Ford and Tesla!
A White Man's Age,
The Age of Amendments,
Income Taxes, Suffrage,
Election by popular vote.
Progressive Age,
The Federal Reserve,
The Trade Commission,
The Eight-hour day,
The League and Peace forever!
Tommy, a Jim Crow segregationist,
A hero to his class, blind to his faults,
Keeping Black Men in the fields.

The Boy, reading in the 50s
Did not recognize the white supremacy
Defining Tom Swift's Eradicate;
Imagined the stars spinning,
Imagined his voyage uncharted,
Cruel and unknown as Amundsen's
Bitter crossing of the Northwest Passage
Or triumphant as the Boy Inventor
In The Caves of Ice?

1920 Harding

His casket entrained,
Superb his rail car,
Millions mourned his sacrifice,
Prudent Gamaliel gone to Oblivion.

Amiable Harding,
Held close the press,
A printer's devil earning his ruler,
Setting type, coveting the editor's page,
His wife indentured to astrologers,
Ensuring his political stars aligned.
Harding, mistress-goaded, a man of fetishes
Addictions and whoring.
The People wearied of Wilson,
His Crusade into the Future,
Flocked to handsome Harding
And his mask of normalcy,
Dark side veiled, a charade.

Elected, taking it to the immigrants,
Then tariffs and tax cuts for the rich,
The catechism of first-term Republicans
For the next hundred years.

Eddie born in 1920,
A recession year,
Mary and Oswald Patrick
Struggling to feed four sons
On mechanic's wages
In the Gatsby Age.

Following Roosevelt and Wilson,
Archangels of progress,
Harding talked of cooperation
In the ashes of the War, a peacemaker.

Campaigning from his Front Porch
America First, then scandals,
Sentences for grifters, grafters, self-dealers,
A team of clown-car criminals, his Ohio friends,
Stealing Veterans' medical supplies,
Selling Naval oil reserves
And passes to White House soirees.
Warren a genial mark for corrupt interests.

Harding dead of heart disease,
Martyred for his Wall Street brothers,
Presidency surrendered to rapacity,
The Market. All hail leverage and deregulation!

His corpse, be-draped, flowered,
Died of natural causes, not Booth's cartridges.
Presented as if Lincoln, savior of the Republic.

Harding, Coolidge and Hoover complicit,
Enriching the white-haired market-makers of '23
Sacrificing the farmers and garment workers of '29.
Witness railroad workers in bread lines,
Machinists crowding soup kitchens
With cups made on their own lathes,
Longshoremen and warehousemen,
Begging for day work,
On ice-slick city corners,
Winter unforgiving in '32.

1923 Coolidge

Delicate Cal freckled and red-haired
Calculating and born cautious
In the Notch between the Green Mountains.
Of the Coolidges who stayed sober
Grinding a living from glacial defiles
And difficult fields opposed to the sun,
While cousins and sisters lit out
For the Northwest Territory,
Leaving farms and debts unattended.

Cal in woolen frock coat doing chores
Channeling his grandfather in that dreamy age
Of Emerson and Thoreau and Self Reliance,
Before the War when men worked as deliberately
As the shy sugar bled from the maples;
Husbanding the land until gone and dead.

Silent Cal, given the staff of office,
Yielded to the ruling class's fixation
On free markets and small government,
Quickly given over to Wall Street accomplices.

Dot born in 1926.
Toddlers, Eddie and Dot,
In those laissez-faire years, the storm coming.
Soon enough, children of the Depression,
Teenagers as War tore up the world.

Coolidge or Chaos in 1924,
Elected on his own,
Adulating Nazi Lindbergh, Aviator,
Deaf to Braintree's Sacco and Vanzetti,

Bank robbers, maybe.
Cal bragging on his surpluses
Blind to Mississippi corpses
From Cairo to Natchez,
Flotsam of the Mississippi Flood.

Cal playing dress-up in the Dakotas
With Borglum, sainted carver of the Black Hills.

Choosing not to run, complicated Cal,
In 1928, a year before the end times.
Cal born on an economic moon tide, fortunate,
And safe in Northampton, diversified.
As president uninterested in regulations,
Indifferent to margin loans and speculation,
Unwilling to prepare the government for war or peace,
Dutiful child of Conservative Values.
The government impotent
When the Coolidge Carousel spun down.
Savage Cal in his New England hubris slept,
A shopkeeper's son to the end,
General of the Economy writing weekly columns,
Praising President Cleveland and the dead warriors of Troy.

1928 Hoover

Bertie, a Band of Hope Quaker,
Orphaned and self-reliant, a plain dresser,
Incarcerated within the machinery of his mind,
Unforgiving and unforgiven, a closed system.

Pirate and Bully, loaner of the people's money,
Like so many other Progressive Saviors
Turning self-confidence and small victories
Into the revelation of conservative zealotry,
Reproving his countrymen, Tyrant,
"I have no plan…going fishing".

Three and nine, Dot and Eddie,
When Bertie turned his back
And ushered in a decade of struggle.
Mary's Oswald, Eddie's dad, repairing cars in Watertown,
Scratching out a living while she cooked for the Bishop.

Charles True, Dot's Dad,
Gone West by '32.
The family dependent on the kindnesses
Of strangers Bertie promised would come.
Dot and her four brothers making do,
On Orange Street, a block from the Watch Factory,
Waltham, Grace at her bench, bent over piecework.

In defeat still deaf to the Depression
His stubbornness intensified,
Conducting the Isolationist Chorus!
Let the Bolsheviks and Social Democrats die
In the Pinsk Marshes, on the banks of the Vistula
On the Budapest Heights—America safe!
Holy Atlantic! Moat of Democracy!

Calling out Hiss and Oppenheimer, Jews
And Women, Students, "Negroes" and Railroad Workers,
The TVA and WPA, Atomic Energy Commission,
FDR, Chambers and Rosenberg,
Methodists, Farmers and Painters, Catholics,
Truman and his United Nations of Socialism,
All conspiring to keep him out.

1932 Roosevelt

From the magic of the radio, authentic verses of hope
From a tenor whose song was heard in kitchens, electrified,
On the factory floor, the melody of the production line,
In the psalms of the field hands beneath straw sunhats,
And hardware store hymnals, men assembled colloquial,
Narratives shared on park benches and oak pews,
A will to act, a call to arms in peace, solidarity in war, a Voice!

Delano's crafting China Trade fortunes,
Hauling opiate cargos to New World harbors
In sharp clippers named for the stars
They sailed by and mythic creatures
That enthralled them,
The craving to let go, surrender
To beasts imagined;
Sailing, until wrecked in wilding storms,
Or abandoned, no longer seaworthy,
Sea Serpent, Surprise, Stag Hound,
Witchcraft, Celestial Empire, Glory of the Seas;
Decades of sailing ships and sailors lost
Serving Hudson River estates,
Upstate Delano and Livingston cousins,
Shiftless, intent on wedding *Mayflower* heiresses.

Sarah, determined to raise another Delano,
Finding in Franklin's father, James,
A man she could love as much as her own father.

Dilettante Franklin, State Senator
Of the Hudson Valley Gentry, riding,
Britches pressed, Poughkeepsie Proletariat,
Promising upstate farmers price supports.

Handsome with Gilded Age pride and pince-nez,
Tone deaf to lower-class suffering
Until cruel Polio proved him mortal.

Franklin working through his infirmities.
In '24 and '28, Eleanor and James Junior
Sustaining the politics and the body,
Franklin climbing the convention canyons,
Crutch and cane, crutch and cane,
James at his elbow, glorious and courageous,
Accepting the pain, useless legs dragged,
Step after step, the convention lectern,
Ascension, Smith nominated!

At Warm Springs, Franklin at the baths,
Eleanor at Val-Kill with her sister
Reformers renewing progressive pledges.
Wheelchairs, Missy at his elbow, a work in progress,
Franklin after those first 30 years of conceit
Still the Boy Scout drinking fetid water,
Polio, like a sentence, his penance.
Eleanor, maturing, a liberal Jeanne d'Arc,
Independent, her own soul in spite of Franklin,
Because of Franklin bearing
The pitiless crosses of the misfortunate,

After Coolidge and Hoover,
Princes of conservative prejudice,
Their Depression, natural selection in practice,
Now, out of GOP excess, Democrat!

War-made, the American Arsenal,
Democratic, the Atlantic poisoned
With U-boats in 1941 hunting,
The Pacific hiding Yamamoto's
Carriers until that Sunday,
When Pearl, battleships anchored,
Accepted twenty-five hundred dead souls,
Vessels and aircraft twisted and smoking.
Franklin shouting Infamy while German
And Italian strongmen gleefully called
The American Fascist bet, believing Franklin,
Liberal and crippled, not up to world war.

Eddie, ruddy, private, twenty-one,
Enlisted December 26, 1941
Two weeks after Pearl, T.H.
Marine 344628, first class.
Four years occupying Pacific islands,
Building concrete bunkers on Tutulia
Coral runways on Nanumea,
2nd Marines, September 1944, crewing
His Browning M-2 .50 caliber gun,
While the Army burned the Japanese out of Angaur
And the Tennessee *shelled the Bowl*
And Dauntless *bombers from the* Wasp *swarmed;*
The survivors in the caves buried alive by bulldozers.
And Eddie's brother Marines died by the hundreds
Within earshot on Peleliu, Eddie manning his Browning,
Eddie, wanting the flamethrower, the M-1, the artless grenade.

New Deal long gone, NRA, PWA
Gone too, Franklin, having saved us all,
WPA and the Fireside Chats,

The Savior of Capitalism
Saving bargaining rights,
Leaving behind the NLRA
SSI, banking reform, farm support,
A government looking beyond
The nostrums of GOP resistance.

Franklin failing in 1944,
Persistent angina and flu,
Struggling to stay focused on the Triad,
The Italian campaign, Overlord,
And the dismembering of Germany.
Dying Franklin surviving, elected.
Inaugurated, a phantom at Yalta,
Soon dead at Warm Springs.

Finally, 1945, with fifty-six dollars and seventy cents
Edie on the Hingham docks discharged
And home to Watertown, soon a milkman,
One of four Patrick boys who served.

Dot, a Ted Williams groupie,
Splendid, indeed!
Graduating high school,
Working in the watch factory by '43,
A stop on his route, his wife by '47.

Americans, remembering his April passing,
So the historians prophesized,
Would fall on naked knees,
Heads bowed, in plangent hymns,

Thanking the spinning spheres
That FDR, American Moses,
Nurtured by Hudson River pharaohs,
Arose to lead the people
Out of tomb-building Egypt.

1945 Truman

Harry capable of Mozart and Armageddon,
Commanding millions across a planet,
Playing Paderewski's minuet,
Demanding noble Nagasaki's incineration.

Railroad paymaster, teller, stockman, farmer, miner, oilman,
Failure too poor for college but a good man so they all said.
Captain of Battery D, firing mustard canisters
Then marrying his childhood sweetheart.

A Mason—like Jackson and Lee,
A man who could plow
His quarter mile furrow straight
With a double team,
The horses negotiating sweeping arcs
As they turned at the top of the section.

So systematic a man—math and music—of pioneers,
Westerner, a climber, a machined cipher,
Working backroom poker tables
And the politics of Southern barbecues,
The anti-Roosevelt, not agile, deliberate,
A careful drinker, who learned the lessons of the frontier,
From men who knew Jesse, or said they did,
Rode with Quantrill, or claimed their Daddy did,
Who took up their broadswords with John Brown
Or chased him back to Harper's Ferry—after bloody Pottawatomie;
Who fought in Jackson County or Lawrence in Bleeding Kansas
The Civil War as real as the prairie-cruel winters
Or the floods before summer soaked up the Missouri
Leaving drought-fired clay fields ceramic.

Clerking for the railroads and banks, unremarkable,
Grant-like in personal failure but the man for the hour
When Franklin, a gazelle in a wheelchair, passed,
Ten pounds of braces yet graceful, almost youthful,

Harry stiffening the backbones of Europe
The Marshall Plan and Resurrection
They've long since forgotten GIs dying
For the centuries of continental crusades.

Eddie and Dot curbside in Watertown,
Waved a flag and urged him to "Give 'em hell"
Willing to vote the Working Man,
Unconvinced by the dissembling Dewey,
Appalled by Segregationist Thurmond,
Or Wallace, the face of Original Sin.

The newsmen stupid with self-fulfilling polling
Too lazy to ask a question and blind to Everyman.

Then '49, the year the Boy was born,
McCarthy and the Hydrogen Bomb,
Card-carrying Communists at State,
NATO created but China lost,
The Red Scare driving political careers.

American Adam out of Jackson County kaolin,
Harry, hard-fired, prairie-made American
Returned to the clay of Independence.
Pioneer who led the world, made good our Promise.
Rugged as the salt-glazed surface of a corn-liquor jug.

1952 Eisenhower

Fortunate Ike, his stars aligned,
River Brethren Bible Reader
Baptized in the Faith of Our Fathers.

Architect of the Middle Way, careful, steady.
To serve his masters, captive of Business,
All sacrificed for consensus.

Carrying MacArthur's baton against the Bonus Army;
Envying Glam Patton's tanks assaulting Memorial Bridge.
Driving the Expeditionary Vets into Maryland.

In '42, Supreme Commander,
Living like an Algerian Pasha,
Morning kisses from his Driver,

In '44, "Okay, we'll go!"
Holding hands with Kay in their caravan
Awaiting the cables from Utah and Omaha.

Armies advancing by the right flank
Across the Normandy fields,
Ike, flagrant with Kay, sunning, the Riviera.

Kay airbrushed from War footage,
Back to London, anonymous.
Ike and Mamie, sunk cost.

For Eddie, the persistence of nightmares
Throughout the Eisenhower years,
When the sun was yellow-hot,

The air wet in late August
In those early morning Nashoba hours
That reminded him of atoll nights
Coast watching in Palau
Surrounded by the dead in coral graves.

Ike, willing to kiss McCarthy's ring.
A smiling man, a man to impress
When in costume and on message.

A cabinet of car dealers
And Plumbers, Dulles and Duller,
Good for GM, Good for America.

Organizing a coup in Iran for British oil barons;
The teenage Khomeini schooled in Sharia
Would survive the Shah to bring Carter to the altar.

And Che, radicalized in Central America,
Fighting with Castro to liberate Cuba,
Become a symbol on flower child Day-Glo posters.

McCarthy on the march hunting Fellow Travelers.
White Councils and Women's Leagues,
Separate but Equal in Post-*Plessy* America.

Warren bent on ending American Apartheid,
Ike, ordering the Airborne to Central High
In Little Rock, in '57.

The Boy all of seven in first grade, chanted,
While the world shifted on its axis,
Oblivious to Cold War currents,

Bussed to school, a playground taunt:
'Whistle while you work, Stevenson's a Jerk
Eisenhower's got the power but he never works.'

The Man, 60 years sober of childhood infatuations,
Thinking Adlai, a talker, a theorist, ideologue
Was never presidential material;
And Ike, probably the man for that Age.

Leaving big decisions for future electors
Eight years of Texas Hold 'Em.
And the promise of Mutual Assured Destruction.

Approving desert testing, deaf to the down-winders,
Too late the pre-Cana counsel against military-industrial marriages
Himself the father of the bride.

The Boy now eleven, sleeping in the broad backseat
Of Eddie's Custom Royal all fins and taillights, black,
Cruising to Plum Island on Sunday morning,
Galvanized pails and clamming sticks stowed.
We Catholics surely damned on the Flats
Searching for quahogs barefoot in the brackish silt
Stepping over tangles of Dead Man's Fingers rotting
And blue-brown helmet-carcasses of Horseshoe Crabs,
Late in the afternoon back to Nashoba, clam buckets
Tarp-covered each side of the drive-shaft bump,
The Dodge slipping like the chromed spaceship
In Forbidden Planet *through a galaxy of traffic.*

Then, Eddie at the table he made from a hollow door,
A riff on a Woodworkers' Illustrated *design;*
The Boy and his father agreeing on one thing:

*Clams in dozens on a Lu-Ray platter, blue,
Steamed and ready for peeling and dipping,
Butter and vinegar in Russell Wright bowls.
Dottie in the den watching the Sullivan show,
In the 50s gloaming normalcy,
In the glow of a presidential smile,
Almost papal, horrors to be unveiled.*

Ike in a plain pine box,
Buried in hardscape Kansas,
General of the Armies, American.

1960 Kennedy

Not his father's first son but Chosen,
Callow boy, colicky, gone to Choate.

The Boy in Nashoba, a sand-pit swimming hole,
Eleven, maybe twelve, saw
A stranger slip without complaint
Into deepening water—at first surprised, resigned—
Until the Boy drug him spitting water, terrorized,
To a sand spar perfect in its grain, red and orange,
Yellowing under the August sun at noon,
Hero, perhaps, not heroic,
The life saved unequal, he guessed, to the lives
Of the sailors Jack saved, storied.

Pretty boy presidency
All Fiddle & Faddle,
Now heroic—balls to the wall,
Missiles in our backyards…the Button.
Jack without mandate, slow to civil rights.
New Freedom, New Deal, New Frontier;
Not FDR, surely, not even Wilson on his best day.

Better Dead than Red, Jack,
Tough on Laos and the Dominoes,
Using the monks' sacrifices,
Paying off Madame Nhu,
Unleashing the Green Berets,
Killers, ignorant of Freedom's trajectory.

The Boy fourteen in the summer of '63
With a permit to work Nashoba farms,
Hectares of Beefstake tomatoes,
Vines hung on miles of steel wire and ash stakes;

Pinching the new suckers in the morning
Alongside island migrants,
Whose names he never learned,
Sheltering in warehouses, summer long,
Behind the apple conveyors, across the parking lot
From St. Elizabeth's, Mass in the cellar,
Communion, despite the stench of apples rotting.

Trucked down to the lower fields behind a huffing tractor,
And on hands and knees, crawling the cornrows
In the murk, beneath the stalks, swaying and crackling,
Like flames in woodfire, airless tunnels, the cow corn
Remorseless, knuckles bleeding, yanking ragweed,
Bindweed and quackgrass from the sun-baked furrows.

Jack never crawled a cornfield,
Pulling weeds, aerating the stalk-beds,
Or sorted McIntosh fruit on the line,
Husbandry not a core requirement at Harvard.
And small town Catholics seldom mingled
With Brookline or Cape Cod congregations
Made up of professional men.

Vietnam and advisors with M1s in their duffels,
Scattered around Delta hamlets chasing the VC.
Diem and the Catholics buying up the countryside
With Kennedy's secret dollars, the Pentagon itching for a fight,
Ho in the North, the Viet Minh waiting.
Corruption and misdirection, Diem, our Diem, Body of Christ.

And November, a perfect day,
From Love Field, the bubble top stowed,
The Lincoln cruising Mockingbird,

Until right on Lemon, right again on Cedar Spring,
Pictures with school girls,
Time for the nuns,
Slowing for the left at the Plaza.

The first shot, a miss, into the granite curb,
Echoing in the Plaza as if multiple shooters:
The grassy knoll,
The picket fence,
The overpass.

Warren's magic bullet through his neck,
"I've been shot!" he said to Jackie,
Grabbing his throat,
The lead already through Connolly.

The third shot, calamity,
An explosion, brain dead,
In Jackie's arms,
Bits of him on her, the car, the Plaza,
The Lincoln rushing to the hospital
Beneath now pitiless banners:
"Welcome To Dallas, Mr. President!"

The Boy in gym class, blue shorts,
White t-shirt, high school.
A slender boy,
Not much of a dodge-baller,
An easy out.
Urgent the return to Home Room,
Hours before last period, no words,
Rumors on the silent ride home,

Bluebird buses, yellow and black,
Ferrying children home to parents in shock.

We are closed because of a death in the Family.

Jackie working on his viewing,
On Lincoln's catafalque, the Coffin,
Bunting smothering the Dome Room.

Reluctant Warren manufacturing the Answer,
Ford rewriting the reports,
Dulles intimidating witnesses:
Oswald crazy in the Annex alone
After Marina drove him to make something of himself.
It's all over now said Oswald, in the basement
Unveiling the smirk that drove Ruby crazy,
Signaling it was time to sell
Whatever story the media might believe.

Jack not worthy of a conspiracy.
After all, what had he concluded?
Another Lincoln focused on mending the nation
Or Garfield—all that promise?
Maybe Manifest McKinley,
Victor of the woeful war with Spain?
After the Bay, no confidence,
The missiles notwithstanding,
No legislation, a runway presidency,
Looking the part, wearing designer rags.

1963 Johnson

A big man from Texas Hill Country,
Tall like his grandmother's men
Cowering in cellars during Comanche Moons;
A dark, moody man hungry for wealth
Like his Johnson namesakes Gone to Texas
Before the war, Kentucky brothers settling the frontier
And scratching the Hill Country limestone,
Grass used-up under hooves of cows gone to Abilene.

Humiliation and heredity, Old Sam Johnson broke
But with friends shrouded in dog-run cabins
In the black land prairies come to bury him
With a yarn about a helping hand
Back in the day in Austin when Lyndon,
Fresh as the rain on the cedar hills, loved him still.

Senator Elect!
Pistoleros voting dead men in worthless Alice;
His Patrón corralling vaqueros with Winchesters,
Buying votes as if bullets for six-shooters,
Box 13 and Landslide Lyndon.

But '63 came,
And power is where power goes!
Johnson, a man tutored by adversity
Promised continuity to the grieving family,
Insisted Civil Rights be the law of the land!
Declaimed a War on Poverty.
Like FDR, willing to act, to govern.
Elected outright, delivering the Great Society,
Voting Rights, Medicare, education reform,

NEA and NASA, Jack's promises realized,
When Johnson, traces striping his shoulders,
Leaned into the ploughshare, forcing the furrow.

By '68, Jack long forgotten,
The flower children promising
To bring Lyndon to heel.
Lying down Lyndon,
Choosing longitudes and latitudes,
For B52s north of the Parallel,
Carpeting the Viet Cong,
Rolling Thunder.
Marines ashore in '65, ten-fold by '68
Despite Sunflower and Mayflower,
Operation Country Fair, Silver Bayonet,
King Fisher and the Phoenix Program,
Viet Cong sacrificed at Khe San, Tet, and Hue,
To soften up the South for Uncle Ho's regulars;
After Niagara, Haiphong,
While diplomats on both sides trolled for advantages,
And "Wise Men" toured Saigon, advised the White House,
The steel rain from the bombers, endless.

The Boy now 18, voting,
Up the back stairs of the Firehouse
Ushered into canvas-covered booths
Handed cardboard ballots and black markers,
The Old Wives, the Acton DAR
Matching their lists in blue ink.
Patrick, Nash Road, Jonathan Clark,
Voting for McCarthy of Minnesota, Poet.
After New Hampshire, Lyndon Nevermore,
First Vote, Democratic, never looked back.

1968 Nixon

A Quaker Boy, awkward, from a lunger family,
A homebody with a Serpent's Tongue,
Always a trimmer, working angles,
One of us, or so he claimed.

Born in the shadow of an eclipse,
So his mother said, years later,
To explain why her Yorba Linda man-child,
Who played in the Anaheim Canal,
Was now so famous despite his failed father.

Maybe he was no more than a burglar, small timer,
A dissolving slick in the Potomac swamp,
Neither Agamemnon, all hubris,
King of the Achaeans, at least,
Nor crafty Caesar, murdered reformer,
Half-naked and dying on the Senate steps
Buried under medieval muck now excavated,
As we lately excavate another Richard
Skeleton twisted, dead from lack of a horse,
From beneath a Leicester car park.

The War all but won in '69
After Tet and the NVA retreat,
When Abrams brought the hammer down,
Stood up the ARVN, brought the fight
To the Cambodian sanctuaries in '70.

The Boy in '68, '69 and '70
Summering in a machine shop,
Timecard diaries recording fractional lives.
Beside laboring men unsaved by deferments,
Dreading the impending draft.

The manufactory fouling the waters of the Assabet,
Raw rusted bars sheared into measured stock,
The hardened steel worked and milled, hammered,
Harvesting knives destined for farm leviathans
The Boy would never see.
The newborn knives gauged
And stacked crosswise,
Carefully, on wooden pallets,
Then punched for mounting studs
By presses from Buffalo and Cincinnati,
Row by row, an Industrial Henge,
Then laid for edges on grinders, sand polished,
Bowed to specification and boxed.
The Boy, a steelworker,
Devouring lunch prepared by Dot,
Always tuna salad, Twinkies
And a can of Coke wrapped in aluminum foil.

Dick, Dick Nixon,
Now Commander-in-Chief
As Kissinger haggled for "peace with honor."
Cluster-bombing the Trail,
B-52s over Laos, the C130 Gunships,
A million dead VC and NVM Regulars
From Vietnam to Cambodia
As the North buckled
Under the warship and airship fusillade,
The ARVN armor and artillery.
Victory was there for the taking!

Winning was no counter to history,
Past or Future.
The US tired of wars and lies,
Our Leader conspiring for an Exit,
Vietnam, unified inevitably.

Tricky Dick joined at the hip to vain Henry
Wandering the Mall at midnight, desperate,
"Don't hate me!" raising the dead at Kent State,
Nixon paying-off Pollster Harris to hammer the liberals.

Then Henry and Dick selling out for '72.
Linebacker Two, wave on wave
Of B-52 Wings and F4 Fighter Bombers.
Punishing the Dragon Court,
The Paris Peace Talks,
South Vietnam factored into the Electoral College.
The Silent Majority, Southern Democrats
And white union bulls, Christians,
Forty-nine states for Dick in '72,
Losing only Massachusetts and South Vietnam.

The Boy, longing for McGovern
In the hating Nixon Years,
Graduated without skills, save language.
In Oblivion, driving his black-and-white Town Taxi,
Ingénu on Boston's antique streets,
A boy from the suburbs, an educated boy,
A debtor, desperate, on his own,
Hacking, oblivious to gentrification
In the years of Bussing, Gas Lines,
Stagflation and Riots, Protests universal;

*Neighborhoods mutilated then
By the iron horror of the Orange Line,
Elevated from Chinatown to Forest Hills;
The Red Line, subterranean,
From privileged Cambridge to abandoned Dorchester;
The Blue Line east and hydra-headed Green Line.
The Boy navigating the punishing metered miles,
Enraged at "keep the change" tips,
Cursing fleet owners, other drivers, the worn-out cars;
Waiting at taxi stands in January blizzards,
Sleet freezing the wipers;
In August, the cab a soul-stealing oven,
Needing to make a $25 nut
For the shift rent, gas and radio.
Cruising for a raised hand, a shout;
At the airport pool, hopeful
For a flat-rate fare and no conversation.
Stomaching the recitations of the sick
On medical treks to Mass General or BCH,
Helping impoverished widows
Negotiate winter-cracked marble stairs
To sub-basement rooms barricaded
Behind steel grates, triple locked,
With the solitary bag of groceries
Social Security allowed each week.
The Boy returning home with $20,
After paying his owners.
And so he labored
Through the twilight of the Age of Nixon.*

The administration confessing
To inoperative statements;
Armed agents seizing Cox's papers,
A coup in the making,
Executive Privilege,
Stonewalling, then faking tape transcripts.
It was all Dean's fault, he lied,
But too many to silence, too many to pay.
A parade of true believers,
All the pretty young men, criminals
Confessing before the Committee.

Dick in exile,
Dictating foreign policy in absentia
In a prideful struggle for redemption,
His Museum carefully constructed,
Personally interpreted, his greatness.
By the 90s in Park Ridge cooking chili,
Plastic Pat, long suffering Thelma Catherine, dead,
Tricia and Julie married off,
A clumsy, angry man to the end.

1974 Ford

Everyman Jerry, capable,
So he told us,
Our Nightmare over,
So he told us
That morning in '75
As Haig and Henry, then Rummy,
Schemed to usurp the presidency,
"For the good of the country,"
And Ronnie, California Brutus,
Whetted the Conservative blade,
Slipped it below the 5th rib
Of footballer Jerry, Healer of the Nation.
Got what he deserved!

Boy Scout Jerry, a joiner,
America Firster, Yalie scion
Of the Republican Diaspora,
Card-carrying Isolationist.

Then Pearl Harbor,
Born Again Internationalist,
Lieutenant Commander Ford, Hero,
Who did his homework, earned it!
From keel laying through war's ending
Mid-shipping the Monterey,
From Wake to the Philippine Sea.

And Eddie in Palau, Saipan, and Tinian;
Fathers and Brothers, Naval gunners and Marines.

A hardworking, earnest Midwesterner,
Coach and Commander, plough horse,
A man suited for Ways and Means, rule-maker.

Honest Jerry,
A man the ambitious could count on,
Transparent, direct, no schemer;
A trusted advisor, moderate.
Jerry, a Pawn in a Bishop's game,
A better man than his Masters,
Sacrificed for Tonkin and Watergate.
But a Nixon Man, no Question,
Happy to snuff political opponents.

Jerry accepting Haig's deal,
Pardon for a criminal
Presidency, paid in full.
Ambition corrupts his affable mask?
Macbeth funneling blistering wax?

WIN, to NYC, Drop Dead!
President Ford, his Neo-Con legacy,
Iraq, Bush I and II, Cheney;
Abetting Greenspan's Ayn Rand infatuation,
His libertarian fortune-telling
Coming full circle in the decades to follow;
Birthing the Boat People, the half-filled helicopters,
Blades beating seaward from Saigon, panicked,
Disgorged hulks toppling into the China Sea.

1976 Carter

Submariner, Commander Carter,
Neither Nixon nor Ford, a Planter,
Resigned to the cross, born again.

In the fields, on their knees, Carters calloused,
Sharing church pews with Klansmen neighbors
Who pursued their own god on the Plains of Dura.

Governor & Lieutenant, washed the stank,
Jimmy, clever Baptist, all JC all the Time.
Striver, striving, hard work its own reward.

Speaking in Tongues Democratic!
Evangelist in a Sinful World, handy,
Pickrick Drumstick Maddox, a hater.

Surely the Lord sent Jimmy
To help the least of us, with chariot
And sword opposing the Sinful World.

'76 and Jimmy who?
A carnival of pretenders—Anybody But Carter—
Bested by the Peanut Brigade.

Walking to the White House, weeping and waving,
Hand in gloved hand with Rosalyn.
The Ministering President, witness!

The Man, married by '77,
Poetry sealed, all technical now.
Reading manuals and white papers.
So many seasons of migrant obscurity

Working the steel and laminate fields
Of word processing workstations,
Longing to be Wallace Stevens,
Lacking his executive perks.

Fishing for copper and purple brim,
Leeches and crawlers on No. 12 barbs.
A man of the people, Jimmy, when home in Georgia.

Hunting for Cherokee points in red clay,
Army worms in the corn and soy.
Playing softball for the tourists.

A man with an ego, presidential,
But bowling in the basement,
After bargaining with Begin.

Jimmy, lusting after the ladies,
Chaste but confessing a wandering eye,
Despite the earthy Georgia beauty of his Rosalyn.

Jimmy righteous in defeat,
Forsaken by the Born Again,
The Moral Majority, who chose an Actor.

Jimmy, an angler,
Both dry and wet fly, a tier,
Counting fall trout, not votes, his Fall.

Striver, betrayed, defeated.
Forgiven, in light of his successors,
Habitats and Nobel notwithstanding.

Cast out by his Evangelical community,
Born again to be martyred atop the City on the Hill,
For safeguarding Civil Rights and Freedom of Choice.

1980 Reagan

Android, a Ken doll turned out
For star-struck fledgling GOP writers
Crafting speeches, opining,
While Central American thugs
Recycled Saudi dollars
In defense of "democratic principles,"
Congress and Constitution be damned,
Ronnie held harmless.

The machinery of history,
Like a belt-driven continuum of looms
Within the water-fed factories
Along the Assabet River
Where the Boy grew up.
Weaving the shawl of exceptionalism
Out of the wool of inequality.

The Boy in Nashoba,
July, sweltering, hopeful,
The Lions Club Fair,
Tents hoisted and staked
In the hardpan acres
North of Mass Ave.,
Surrounding the Pit
Where he swam before the August algae
Turned the spring-fed water to green sludge.
The Boy knew many Ronnies
Manning the ring toss, the galleries,
The cigarette bets, holding the tent cloths,
Promising revelations, a peek,
Selling precious tickets to witness
Mermaids and sisters conjoined,

Five-hoofed cows, three-headed dogs.
The Ronnies of the world,
Toothy smiles, blackened-hair, selling
The persistence of the Republican Rapture.

Mother Nell, sainted.
Father Jack dead drunk.
Little Dutch temporizing
Frank Merriwell fables,
Dime-store novels, his stock, his trade.

Ronnie, FBI informant T-10,
Dropping a dime on fellow actors, all "commies;"
Loyal only to his script,
Carrying water for studio management
And corrupt union bosses,
A part in a play, a line, stage right.

Casting couch Nancy, Bride.

Spear carrier for Electrical Living,
The Road Ahead applianced,
Emblazoned with the GE badge, More Good Done.
Ronnie fired from his cushy job,
Famous, dressed in his ideology,
Content to be the New Right's mannequin.
Nancy dressing him for office,
The tilt of the head, the wry smile,
The twinkle in the those hazel eyes
That betrayed him, Actor.

Nancy knowing the score
And protecting early onset Ronnie,
A year or two from incoherence
At Reykjavik, cue cards falling
From palsied fingers,
Talking points, so exquisitely authored,
Aflutter, helter-skelter falling
Between his snakeskin cowboy boots.

And the Boy, now an Old Man,
Searching scrapbooks he saved
Documenting Ronnie's decade,
Newspapers witnessing
The wedge of class warfare.
An edge beaten cold on a Republican forge,
The hammer keen, the anvil loud,
Blacksmiths of white hate, believers,
The Republican 80s ensuring decades
Of dysfunction, disinformation,
Discrimination and debt,
Government disabled, the People ungoverned.

Wild Bill Casey mumbling about Contra funding
Ollie North saluting: USA, USA, USA!
Marines buried in Beirut rubble;
And the march of corrupt officials endless,
Teflon, Liar, Ronnie asleep at the switch,
The Fellas deciding, in charge not elected.

1984, demented Ronnie re-crowned,
'There you go again…' debated.
Deficits and Taxes, making it up in speeches
Nancy and Astrologers dictating Calendars.

The Boy, his poetry gone,
On a corporate ladder learning his craft.

Blood & Guts Ollie docked before Congress,
Ronnie in Oval Office speeches dishonest:
"I knew nothing, of course, about arms for hostages."

1988 Bush

Herbert Walker, Flyboy Hero,
Prescott and Bush,
A grey-suited plain man
Out of the Mass Bay Colony,
Patrician Faustus in Texas,
Lacking "the Vision Thing."

All resume, no soul,
Hard working New Englander!
Fallen moderate,
Avatar Avenger plummeting
Into the Philippine Sea aflame,
Bush Agonistes, co-pilot dead.
Moralist and preacher, no pulpit,
Program or platform,
Wingless and rescued
For service in a world
Where ideology guts knowledge,
Herbert Walker, apparatchik.

Anybody But Bush!
Yet, it all worked out,
History being what it is,
Independent of Presidents
And First Ladies
And Compacts made in bleak Massachusetts Bay,
Mayflower, beached on the hard-hearted,
Pequot shore.

"Read my lips!" bragged George
While Atwater pissed in every well,
Poisoned the political discourse,

Worked on realizing the worst in all of us,
Willie in that turnstile, Willie, Willie, Willie.

Silent George now President,
"I'm the Man!"
The USSR in free fall,
George a helpless accomplice
To German Unification
And the reduction to Mother Russia.
"This will not Stand!" Kuwait in flames.
Clarence and hearings as spectacle.
Cheney in the backroom planning Armageddon.

And defeat Stupid!
"I let everyone down!"
Surely, but it was the economy,
Stupid, and you had no story to tell,
Except Fountain speedboats,
Maine palaces and Springers,
Mother Barbara, prim and positive,
Awash with Pilgrim's Progress remedies.
The Mayflower nostrums unimportant
To the Kennebunk house-poor
Employed, unnamed, to clean and mow,
To cook or split firewood, to drive,
To make good and calm Bush lives,
Remaking the few and precious minutes
Before dawn, before the Northeast wind
Rises up and the bay waters
Stretch perfectly green-blue to the east.

So much the GOP could not do
After the usurper Clinton
Put an end to Honor, Duty and Country.

The Man conflicted, longing
To unleash lightning in his verses,
Confessing upon reflection
That George, a victim in a Captivity Narrative,
Did not deserve the curses,
Last of his generation, a twilight figure,
Raised to serve, Served.
The Man, upon the Aviator's passing,
Felt surprise at his disappointment,
Regret that a story heroic unraveled,
One more voice dumbed down.

1992 Clinton

Hope waned and waxed
In William Jefferson Clinton,
All flesh-cursed his genius,
Manifest his weaknesses
For brunette temptresses.
Tragic his penance,
Decades upon the wrack
Of Right Wing conspiracies
Real and imagined.

A boy with no limits,
Born to run, spoiled,
Virginia in every kiss,
Roger in every fist.
Perfected politician,
Imperfect husband
Wanting poesies, a weeper,
Wearing the hair shirt,
Wanting the cane,
Hillary his Chorus.

Bill Blythe, father?
Suicide by Buick
And Bourbon, speeding South
The convenient father of a president,
Dead in a ditch off I-55.

'92 and campaigning,
All white Arkansan Bill
Building his brand,
Bringing the hammer down
On Sister Souljah,

Approving Ricky Ray Rector's last meal,
The pecan pie saved for later.

Elected! White House chaotic,
Puerile Steph, partisan,
Bosnia and budget wars.
The despot Gingrich,
The criminal Milosevic,
The application of Deliberate Force,
By White House dilettantes.

Bill bringing the cold steel down
On training camps in Afghanistan
And Sudanese pharma factories
To distract from his red-faced
Lying about Monica, dark-haired,
Her dress, blue, couplings
Beneath the Desk Resolute.
So, Operation Infinite Reach,
So, Wag the Dog.
Dodger, lacking the moral authority,
To command the armies when Chief.
The Croats, Serbs and Bosnians unified
Under the shadow of a B-52 Wing,
In the peace of carpet bombing.

Confessor Bill penitent
As Right-Wing cabalists
Invented indiscretions in handshakes,
Hugs or rope-line exchanges.
Bloodied by impeachment.
Bill besotted, surely sinful,
But innocent of high crimes.

The Man, Democrat!
Abhorring the Republican Contract,
Compared their transgressions
To Clinton, a dog,
Profoundly disappointing
A predator, a damaged soul,
A man with needs, a man who leads.

2000 Bush

W. gifted the Presidency
By his Father's man, Lawyer Baker,
Rehnquist ex Machina.

The Man in November, 2000,
Binging on the election, media-raptured,
The popular vote won!
Except beleaguered Gore,
His challenge halfhearted, unconvincing;
Our fates determined by bloodless Justices
Issuing injunctions against hanging chads,
Rescript for Oblivion, our Court's decisions.
The Man blaming toothless Gore,
Not demanding the full Florida recount
While volunteer poll workers
In Broward floundered
Before reporters' cameras and the nation,
Inspecting ballots under magnifying glasses,
Paid observers sowing doubt and confusion,
The People distracted and denied.

Naive, the Man believed
Presidents, challenged, would rise.
That there was a Lincoln
Or Roosevelt in everyman.
In the crawl of months and years
After that macabre September morning,
W. found reading children's stories,
Cheney assuming command
Bunkered beneath the White House,
Pentagon blackened and Towers imploded,
The Man, wanting a Hero for his time,
Surely One would come.

The Neo-cons empowered went to war,
Pompous Rumsfeld's snowflakes,
Dumbed down, the Baghdad rush,
Yellow Cake and Aluminum Rods,
Deceiver and Decider
Needing to hit the evil-doers hard.

Saddam too proud to tell the truth,
Oz in Mesopotamia,
Demanding decades of sacrifice,
A culture broken, ancient Assyria in tears.

In the carnage of Samawah
And the bridges of Nasiriyah,
American Plantagenet Bush vainglorious.

No plan for the Fedayeen in their Toyotas,
In the orange haze of the chamal,
Firing from mosques and madrassas,
Veiled by Red Crescent, defilade,
The burqas of their sisters and daughters.

Where was the love?
The welcoming freedom fighters?

Warheads on foreheads,
And Mission Accomplished,
Six weeks in, Saddam in the wind,
Occupiers, nation-building in Baghdad, Mosul, Tikrit,
The British cautious in Basra, but Anbar,
Holy Anbar! No peacekeeping in Fallujah.

Four more years of wreck and ruin
Markets free falling, Bush helpless,
Billions sacrificed after billions
Redistributed in another Republican
Financial misadventure
Loosed upon the populace
By Laffer Curve believers,
Accepting the mythic napkin sketch,
As if the Holy Face on the Turin Shroud.

And, the bio-labs, a lie.
The yellow cake, a lie.
The aluminum tubes, a lie.
Liberators, a lie, a lie, a damned lie.

2008 Epilogue Obama

November dark, drunk
On Syrah and Hurrahs.
Wanton the moonlight,
Anchorless the studio,
Woozily the pond sopping
The foot of the hill,
As I, almost 60,
Amateur pundit,
Wanderer, I alone, unwinding,
Shadowed beneath the impenetrable limbs
Of coast live oaks two hundred years growing
Sporadic with fireflies, humming with cicadas.
Crickets hidden in the lichened roots,
The harmonics of millions murmuring,
He won, the landslide!
The millions susurrating,
Washington's white ruins,
I alone…One…Voter!
The millions and millions,
The atoms composed,
The cicada's instrument
Informing the oak's verticality,
Liquefying the chilled air flowing.
Smoldering in the spinning stars
The millions of us
He won…the landslide!

Bibliography

Alighieri, Dante. 1901. *The Divine Comedy of Dante Aligheiri.* Translated by Henry Wordsworth Longfellow. New York, P. F. Collier.

Alter, Jonathan. 2007. *The Defining Moment : FDR's Hundred Days and the Triumph of Hope.* New York: Simon & Schuster Paperbacks.

Ambrose, Stephen E. 1988. *Nixon Volume I: The Education of a Politician 1913 – 1962.* Simon & Schuster.

———. 1991. *Nixon Volume II: The Triumph of a Politician 1962 – 1972.* Simon & Schuster.

———. 1992. *Nixon Volume III: Ruin and Recovery 1973 – 1990.* Simon & Schuster.

Anand Giridharadas. 2019. *Winners Take All.* Random House USA.

Andersen, Kurt. 2018. *Fantasyland : How America Went Haywire : A 500-Year History.* London: Ebury Press.

Ayers, Edward L. 2018. *The Thin Light of Freedom : The Civil War and Emancipation in the Heart of America.* New York, NY: W. W. Norton & Company.

Beevor, Antony. 2014. *The Second World War.* London Phoenix.

Benner, Erica. 2018. *BE LIKE THE FOX : Machiavelli in His World.* S.L.: W.W Norton.

Blight, David W. 2019. *FREDERICK DOUGLASS : Prophet of Freedom.* S.L.: Simon & Schuster.

Bliss, Sylvester, and George R Knight. 2005. *Memoirs of William Miller.* Berrien Springs, Mich.: Andrews University Press.

Brands, H W. 2013. *Traitor to His Class: The Privileged Life and Radical Presidency of Franklin Delano Roosevelt*. New York, Anchor Books.

Bowden, Mark. 2018. *Huế 1968 : A Turning Point of the American War in Vietnam*. New York: Atlantic Monthly Press.

Burton, David H. 2004. *William Howard Taft : Confident Peacemaker*. New York, New York: Fordham University Press Philadelphia, Pennsylvania: Saint Joseph's University Press.

Cannon, James M. 2013. *Gerald R. Ford : An Honorable Life*. Ann Arbor: Univ. Of Michigan Press.

Carter, Jimmy. 2011. *White House Diary*. New York: Picador Usa.

Catton, Bruce. 1961. *The Coming Fury*. Garden City: Doubleday.

———. 1963. *Terrible Swift Sword*. Garden City, N.Y.: Doubleday.

———. 1965. *Never Call Retreat*. New York: Doubleday & Co.

Charles Bracelen Flood. 2012. *Grant's Final Victory : Ulysses S. Grant's Heroic Last Year*. Boston, Ma: Da Capo Press.

Chivers, C J. 2019. *The Fighters : Americans in Combat in Afghanistan and Iraq*. New York: Simon & Schuster.

Chua, Amy. 2018. *Political Tribes : Group Instinct and the Fate of Nations*. New York, New York: Penguin Press, An Imprint Of Penguin Random House Llc.

Coates, Ta-Nehisi. 2017. *We Were Eight Years in Power : An American Tragedy*. London: Hamish Hamilton.

Cooper, John Milton. 2011. *Woodrow Wilson : A Biography*. New York: Vintage Books.

Cozzens, Peter. 2016. *EARTH IS WEEPING : The Epic Story of the Indian Wars for the American West.* Alfred A. Knopf.

Crowley, Monica. 1998. *Nixon in Winter.* New York: Random House.

Dallek, Robert. 2007. *Nixon and Kissinger : Partners in Power.* New York: Harpercollins Pub.

———. 2018. *Franklin D. Roosevelt : A Political Life.* New York: Penguin Books.

———. 2020. *How Did We Get Here? : From Theodore Roosevelt to Donald Trump.* New York: Harper, An Imprint Of Harper Collins Publishers.

Dante, Aligheiri. 1994. *The Divine Comedy – Translated by Henry Wadsworth Longfellow.* Grolier Enterprise.

Donald, David Herbert Donald. 1996. *Lincoln.* Norwalk, Conn.: Easton Press.

Dean, John W. 2004. *Warren G. Harding.* New York: Times Books.

Ehrman, Bart D. 2019. *The Triumph of Christianity : How a Forbidden Religion Swept the World.* New York: Simon & Schuster Paperbacks.

Eizenstat, Stuart, and Madeleine Korbel Albright. 2018. *President Carter : The White House Years.* New York, New York: Thomas Dunne Books, St. Martin's Press.

Fehrenbach, T R. 2008. *This Kind of War : The Classic Korean War History.* Dulles, Va.: Potomac Books.

Ferreiro, Larrie D. 2017. *Brothers at Arms : American Independence and the Men of France and Spain Who Saved It*. New York: Vintage Books, A Division Of Penguin Random House LLC.

Foner, Eric. 2012. *The Fiery Trial : Abraham Lincoln and American Slavery*. New York ; London: W.W. Norton.

———. 1988. *Reconstruction: America's Unfinished Revolution, 1863 – 1877*. New York, Harper & Row.

Freeman, Joshua B. 2019. *BEHEMOTH : A History of the Factory and the Making of the Modern World*. W. W. Norton & Company.

Gartner, John D. 2009. *In Search of Bill Clinton*. New York: Griffin ; Godalming.

Goodell, Jeff. 2018. *The Water Will Come : Rising Seas, Sinking Cities, and the Remaking of the Civilized World*. Carlton, Vic.: Black Inc.

Gordon, Michael R, and Bernard E Trainor. 2007. *Cobra II : The inside Story of the Invasion and Occupation of Iraq*. New York: Vintage Books.

Gould, Lewis L. 2014. *Chief Executive to Chief Justice : Taft Betwixt the White House and Supreme Court*. Lawrence (Kan.): University Press Of Kansas, Cop.

Grant, Ulysses S. 1885. *Personal Memoirs of U. S. Grant. In Two Volumes*. New York: C. L. Webster.

Greenberger, Scott S. 2019. *UNEXPECTED PRESIDENT: The Life and Times of Chester A. Arthur*. Hatchett Books.

Groom, Winston, and National Geographic Society (U.S. 2013. *Shiloh, 1862*. Washington, D.C.: National Geographic Society.

H Paul Jeffers. 2002. *An Honest President : The Life and Presidencies of Grover Cleveland*. New York: Perennial.

Harry Joseph Sievers. 1996a. *Benjamin Harrison, Hoosier President*. Indianapolis: American Political Biography Press.

———. 1996b. *Benjamin Harrison Hoosier Statesman*. Newtown, Ct.: American Political Biography Press.

———. 1996c. *Benjamin Harrison Hoosier Warrior*. Newtown, Ct.: American Political Biography Press.

Hastings, Max. 2009. *Retribution : The Battle for Japan, 1944–45*. New York: Vintage.

———. 2018. *Vietnam : An Epic Tragedy : 1945 – 1975*. London: William Collins.

Henley, Patricia. 2000. *Hummingbird House*. Denver: Macmurray & Beck.

Hess, Earl J. 2016. *Braxton Bragg : The Most Hated Man of the Confederacy*. Chapel Hill: The University Of North Carolina Press.

Hitchens, Christopher, and Douglas Brinkley. 2014. *No One Left to Lie to : The Triangulations of William Jefferson Clinton*. London: Atlantic Books.

Hoganson, Kristin L. 2020. *HEARTLAND : An American History*. S.L.: Penguin Books.

Hoover, Herbert, and George H Nash. 2011. *Freedom Betrayed : Herbert Hoover's Secret History of the Second World War and Its Aftermath.* Stanford, California: Hoover Institution Press, Stanford University.

Isikoff, Michael, and David Corn. 2007. *Hubris : The inside Story of Spin, Scandal, and the Selling of the Iraq War.* New York: Three Rivers Press.

Jean Edward Smith. 2008. *FDR.* New York: Random House Trade Paperbacks.

———. 2013. *Eisenhower : In War and Peace.* New York: Random House.

———. 2017. *Bush.* New York: Simon & Schuster.

Jeremi Suri. 2017. *The Impossible Presidency : The Rise and Fall of America's Highest Office.* New York: Basic Books.

Jones, Jacqueline. 2017. *Goddess of Anarchy : The Life and Times of Lucy Parsons, American Radical.* New York: Basic Books.

Karnow, Stanley. 1991. *Vietnam : A History.* New York, New York: Viking.

Keegan, John. 2005. *The Iraq War.* London: Pimlico.

Kershaw, Ian. 2099. *TO HELL AND BACK : Europe, 1914 – 1949.* S.L.: Allen Lane.

Klein, Joe. 2003. *The Natural : The Misunderstood Presidency of Bill Clinton.* New York: Broadway Books.

Lachman, Charles. 2011. *A Secret Life : The Sex, Lies, and Scandal of Grover Cleveland's Presidency.* Skyhorse Pub Co Inc.

Leuchtenburg, William E. 2009. *Herbert Hoover*. New York: Times Books.

Longacre, Edward. 2007. *General Ulysses s. Grant - the Soldier and the Man.* The Perseus Books Group.

McCullough, David. 1992. *Truman*. NY: Simon & Schuster.

———. 2020. *PIONEERS : The Heroic Story of the Settlers Who Brought the American Ideal West.* S.L.: Simon & Schuster.

McDonough James Lee. 2017. *WILLIAM TECUMSEH SHERMAN : In the Service of My Country*. W W Norton.

McPherson, James M. 2003. *Battle Cry of Freedom : The Civil War Era.* New York: Oxford University Press

Meacham, Jon. 2008. *The American Lion*. Random House.

———. 2016. *Destiny and Power.* Random House Usa Inc.

———. 2019. *The Soul of America : The Battle for Our Better Angels*. New York: Random House.

Meyer, G J. 2015. *A World Undone : The Story of the Great War, 1914 – 1918*. New York: Bantam Dell.

Miller, Scott. 2013. *The President and the Assassin : McKinley, Terror, and Empire at the Dawn of the American Century.* New York: Random House.

Milton, John. 2016. *Paradise Lost & Paradise Regained.* Brantford, Ontario: W. Ross Macdonald School Resource Services Library.

Morris, Adam. 2019. *American Messiahs : False Prophets of a Damned Nation*. New York: Liveright Publishing Corporation, A Division Of W. W. Norton & Company.

Morris, Edmund. 2010a. *The Rise of Theodore Roosevelt*. New York: Random House.

———. 2010b. *Theodore Rex*. New York: Random House Trade Paperbacks.

———. 2011. *Colonel Roosevelt*. New York: Random House.

Newton, Jim. 2012. *Eisenhower : The White House Years*. New York: Anchor Books, A Division Of Random House, Inc.

Nicolson, Adam. 2015. *Why Homer Matters*. New York: Picador/Henry Holt And Company.

Pafford, John M. 2019. *Chester A. Arthur : The Accidental President*. Washington, DC, Regnery History,

Paul Anthony Rahe. 2017. *The Grand Strategy of Classical Sparta : The Persian Challenge*. New Haven: Yale University Press.

Perlstein, Rick. 2008. *Nixonland : The Rise of a President and the Fracturing of America*. New York: Simon & Schuster.

———. 2015. *The Invisible Bridge : The Fall of Nixon and the Rise of Reagan*. New York: Simon & Schuster.

Pringle, Henry F. 2017. *William Howard Taft : The Life and Times*. Vol. One. New Town, Connecticut: Published By American Political Biography Press.

———. 2017. *William Howard Taft : The Life and Times*. Vol. Two. New Town, Connecticut: Published By American Political Biography Press.

Randall Herbert Balmer. 2014. *Redeemer : The Life of Jimmy Carter*. New York: Basic Books, A Member Of The Perseus Books Group.

Reeves, Richard. 2007. *President Reagan : The Triumph of Imagination*. London: Simon & Schuster.

Reynolds, David S. 1995. Walt Whitman's America : A Cultural Biography. New York: Knopf.

———. 2020. Abe: Abraham Lincoln in His Times. New York, Penguin Press.

Robert Kincaid Murray. 1969. *The Harding Era : Warren G. Harding and His Administration*. Minneapolis: University Of Minnesota Press.

Robinson, Marilynne. 2019. *What Are We Doing Here?* Toronto: McClelland & Stewart.

Sabato, Larry. 2014. *Kennedy Half-Century : The Presidency, Assassination, and Lasting Legacy of John F. Kennedy*. New York: Bloomsbury.

Shlaes, Amity. 2014. *Coolidge*. New York, Ny: Harper Perennial.

Shorto, Russell. 2018. *Revolution Song : A Story of American Freedom*. New York: W.W. Norton & Company.

Simon, James F. 2006. *Lincoln and Chief Justice Taney : Slavery, Secession, and the President's War Powers*. New York, New York: Simon & Schuster.

Sobel, Robert. 2015. *Coolidge : An American Enigma.* Washington, D.C.: Regnery Publishing.

Sorley, Lewis. 2006. *A Better War : The Unexamined Victories and Final Tragedy of America's Last Years in Vietnam.* San Diego: Harcourt, [Post], Cop.

Stiles, E. J. 2009. *The First Tycoon.* Random House.

Taliaferro, John. 2014. *All the Great Prizes : The Life of John Hay, from Lincoln to Roosevelt.* New York ; London ; Toronto ; Sydney ; New Delhi: Simon Et Schuster Paperbacks May.

Toll, Ian W. 2012. *Pacific Crucible : War at Sea in the Pacific, 1941 – 1942.* New York, New York: W.W. Norton.

———. 2016. *The Conquering Tide : War in the Pacific Islands, 1942 – 1944.* New York, New York: W.W. Norton & Company.

———. 2020. *Twilight of the Gods: War in the Western Pacific, 1944 – 1945.* New York, New York: W.W. Norton & Company.

Trefousse, Hans. 2002. *Rutherford B. Hayes.* Henry Holt and Company, LLC.

Walt Whitman, and Emory Holloway. 1942. *Leaves of Grass : The Collected Poems of Walt Whitman.* New York: Book League Of America.

White, Ronald C. 2009. *A. Lincoln : A Biography.* New York: Random House.

Winkler, Adam. 2019. *We the Corporations : How American Businesses Won Their Civil Rights.* New York: Liveright Publishing Corporation.

About the Author

Jonathan Clark Patrick's fascination with the American presidency began during his childhood in the region around Boston, where so many key events in U.S. political history have occurred. He now resides in the San Francisco Bay area with his wife of forty-five years. Patrick drove a cab during graduate school, writing his first poems while studying American literature. He put aside his writing as he became more successful in his professional services career. Inspired by the momentous 2008 election, Patrick returned in *Songs Presidential* to his lifelong goal of exploring the interaction between history and poetry.

www.ingramcontent.com/pod-product-compliance
Lightning Source LLC
Chambersburg PA
CBHW032006080426
42735CB00007B/527